SILENT LAUGHTER

by

Billy Van Zandt

&

Jane Milmore

SAMUEL FRENCH, INC.

45 West 25th Street
NEW YORK 10010
LONDON

7623 Sunset Boulevard
HOLLYWOOD 90046
TORONTO

ISBN 0 573 60280 8 Printed in U.S.A. #21509

IMPORTANT BILLING AND CREDIT REQUIREMENTS

All producers of **SILENT LAUGHTER** must give credit to the Author of the Play in all programs distributed in connection with performances of the Play, and in all instances in which the title of the Play appears for the purposes of advertising, publicizing or otherwise exploiting the Play and /or a production. The name of the Author must appear on a separate line on which no other name appears, immediately following the title and must appear in size of type not less than fifty percent of the size of the title type.

"SILENT LAUGHTER" opened Off-Broadway at the Lamb's Theatre on Thursday March 18, 2004. It was produced by Carolyn Rossi-Copeland. It was directed by Billy Van Zandt. Associate Director was Robert Ross Parker. Set design was by Dana Kenn. Lighting design was by Richard Winkler. Costume design was by Cynthia Nordstrom. Production Stage Manager was Thom Schilling. Assistant Stage Manager was Jason Sutton. General Managers were Nancy Nagel Gibbs and Lawrence Anderson for NJNG Productions. Press Representative was Keith Sherman and Associates. Marketing was by Leanne Schanzer. Advertising was by the Eliran Murphy Group. Legal services by Sendroff and Associates. Photography by Carol Rosegg. Company Manager was Laura Kirspel. The Organist and Composer was Ralph Ringstad Jr.

THE CAST
(In Order of Appearance)

Brewster Thickwad III	KEN JENNINGS
Lovestruck Woman	MEGAN BYRNE
Lovestruck Man	ED CARLO
Sarge	ART NEILL
Vendor	JIM FITZPATRICK
Drunk	JAMES DARRAH
Billy	BILLY VAN ZANDT
Billy's Pal	GLENN JONES
Ruth	JANE MILMORE
Fat Lady	JAMES DARRAH
Lionel	JOHN GREGORIO
Janitor	JIM FITZPATRICK
Worker	ED CARLO
Worker	JAMES DARRAH
Max the Thug	KEN JENNINGS
Man with Fruitcake	ED CARLO
Cop	MEGAN BYRNE

Cop	ED CARLO
Cop	JAMES DARRAH
Dowager	JIM FITZPATRICK
Butler	JIM FITZPATRICK
Prisoner	MEGAN BYRNE
Prisoner	ED CARLO
Prisoner	JAMES DARRAH
Max's Dame	MEGAN BYRNE
Priest	JIM FITZPATRICK
Maitre D'	KEN JENNINGS
Singing Waiter	JAMES DARRAH
Newsboy	KEN JENNINGS
Recruiter	MEGAN BYRNE
Old Bearded Man	JIM FITZPATRICK
Old One-Armed Man	MEGAN BYRNE
Solder	ED CARLO
Soldier	JAMES DARRAH
Enemy Soldier	MEGAN BYRNE
Bridesmaid	MEGAN BYRNE
Baker	JAMES DARRAH
Understudies	IAN GONZALEZ
	ELLIE MOONEY

CAST OF CHARACTERS

BILLY...the Hero

RUTH...his Heroine

BILLY'S PAL...his Pal

LIONEL DRIPPINWITHIT...his Arch-Enemy

BREWSTER THICKWAD...his Boss and Future Father-in-Law

MAX the THUG...his Cellmate and Foxhole Buddy

SARGE...his Nemesis

And a Cast of Hundreds

AUTHORS' NOTE

"Silent Laughter" is a silent movie performed live onstage.

The sets, props and costumes are done in varying shades of grey, black and white.

Photographs of 1917 New York City are projected on a rear screen for each scene's action.

Super titles over the actor's heads supply the dialogue.

A full score played on a theater organ accompanies the play.

(CURTAIN RISES. ORGANIST OVERTURE.)

Over the opening credits to the silent film "Silent Laughter," we hear a quick medley of the film score. At the conclusion of the overture, the screen rises revealing a tableau of New York City life, 1917.

Over the audience's heads we see a auper-title, done in B & W old-fashioned script.

Title Card #1: "New York City, 1917."

(REAR SCREEN PROJECTION: NYC STREET, POOR SIDE OF TOWN)
SUGGESTED MUSIC: "EAST SIDE, WEST SIDE"

The action begins. A young woman follows her hat as it blows across the street. A young man coming the other way picks it up. They gaze into each other's eyes, fall in love and EXIT together. A cop on the beat *("SARGE")* tips his hat to a rich tycoon. A vendor sets up his wares. From underneath the stockade fence rolls out a down-on-his-luck tramp named Billy.

(SUGGESTED MUSIC: BILLY'S THEME.)

Title Card #2: "Billy – So poor, nail biting isn't a bad habit. It's dinner!"

This hole behind the fence is his home. He wears ill-fitting clothes and a crushed hat. He's cold and starving. He yawns, cleans his teeth with his finger, and scratches his butt. Now he is ready to start the day.

Billy smells the vendor's food. Billy asks if he can spare a crumb to eat. The vendor asks for money. Billy doesn't have any. The vendor reacts - pushing him away, cursing a bluestreak. A beat after he finishes:

Title Card #3: "Beat it!"

The vendor goes back to his cart. Billy looks around to make sure no one is watching, and as the vendor bends down to get something behind his cart, Billy steals a pastry off the cart, which he quickly eats. The vendor rises from beneath the cart, and shakes his head – he's sure he had more cakes on the cart, but shrugs.

The vendor bends down to get a fork, and Billy steals a second pastry, which he stuffs in his mouth. The vendor reacts to another missing cake.

The vendor looks at the plate again, scratching his head. He leans in to look at the plate closer, raises it to look underneath the plate for holes and then turns around – plate in hand – checking the ground to see where the cakes could have gone, Billy looks at the ground turning in the opposite direction and steals and eats a third cake as they pass each other mid-turn.

The vendor gives Billy the eye and moves the plate to the left side of the counter and turns away to take out a link of sausages. Billy leans towards the plate to steal another cake, but the vendor turns around catching Billy with his arm out-stretched. Billy pretends to be swatting at a fly – ending up with the fly "swatted" on the vendor's forehead.

Billy moves to the left and stomps "the dead fly" on the ground. The vendor crosses down to look at the invisible crushed bug, Billy crosses back, stealing a fourth cake. The vendor reacts to the missing cake.

As the vendor bends down for a frying pan, Billy steals a fifth cake. He eats it and goes for a sixth cake, which empties the plate.

("SARGE" ENTERS, catching BILLY.)

Billy reacts then offers the Sarge the last cake. Sarge raises his night stick as Billy jumps away. Sarge, grabbing at Billy, jumps into the same position Billy was in. Simultaneously, the vendor whips around and clubs Sarge in the face with a frying pan, mistaking him for Billy.

Vendor takes his cart and high-tails it out of there. Sarge rises and chases Billy who stuffs sausages he just stole down his pants.

They round the fence. They round the fence a second time. Running between them is Billy's Pal.

Title Card #4: "Billy's Pal."

(They jump in the air, turn to S.R. and start running in place. REAR SCREEN PROJECTION: THE STREET SCENE MOVES OFF.)

As the threesome run in place, the image of the poor side of town moves off L along with the fence.

Billy's Pal eats a bruised banana, and drops the peel. The peel and Sarge go flying off L. Billy and Billy's Pal stop running. They jump in the air.

(REAR SCREEN PROJECTION: THE STREET SCENE STOPS MOVING.)

Billy and his pal run off R.

Blackout

(SUGGESTED MUSIC CUE: HEROINE MUSIC - RUTH'S THEME.)

Title Card #5: "Meet Ruth. Sweet and beautiful. Rumor has it she's double-jointed."

(REAR SCREEN PROJECTION: NYC STREET – NICE PART OF TOWN.)

We see Ruth, a rich man's daughter, walking down the street. She meets a fat lady with a baby in a wicker pram. Ruth coochie-coos the baby.

Title Card #6: "Is it a boy or a girl?"

Ruth coochie-coos again and a continuous spritz of water squirts up from the pram into Ruth's face.

Title Card #7: "A boy."

Ruth reacts.

(SUGGESTED MUSIC CUE: VILLAIN MUSIC.)

Lionel Drippinwithit slinks in from S.R.

Title Card #8: "Lionel Drippinwithit. He has eyes for Ruth. And hands for everyone else."

He meets up with and flirts with Ruth. He is a gentleman dandy, and a real sleaze. Lionel coochie-coos the baby Ruth is looking at. And when she and the fat lady turn away to talk, he flicks ashes from his cigar onto the baby in the pram. Ruth and the fat lady turn back because the baby is now crying. Lionel plays innocent. The fat lady turns in a huff and exits with the pram. Lionel goes to grab her ample bum but restrains himself. Instead, he tips his hat to Ruth and says:

Title Card #9: "I'll be sure to say hello to your father, Ruth!"

Lionel exits crossing behind Ruth and goosing her in the process. He fixes his ring as he EXITS. Ruth watches him suspiciously and waves until he exits.

Ruth turns to cross S.R. just as Billy and his pal run on S.R. to S.L. looking back over their shoulders. They smash into Ruth. They look down to Billy's lap. They look out in surprise. Billy pulls out a string of sausages from his D.S. pocket. Ruth is relieved. Billy is embarrassed and tosses the sausages off. Billy's Pal follows the sausages off.

(SUGGESTED MUSIC CUE: LOVE THEME)

Ruth makes eyes at Billy - love at first sight. Billy makes eyes at her. She acts coy, her finger in her mouth, rocking back and forth. He does too. Ruth sways back and forth acting shy. Billy does too. Ruth introduces herself. Billy tips his hat and introduces himself Ruth says:

Title Card #10: "I feel as if we've met. Do you ever dine at Keen's Chophouse?"

Billy is embarrassed to say no. He pulls his pockets out, explaining he's broke. Ruth pats him sympathetically. Billy's Pal re-enters and pats him as well.

Title Card #11: "My father is Brewster Thickwad III. He owns the screw factory. Tell him I sent you and I'm sure he'll give you a job."

Billy gets excited, lifting his hat in the air with two hands. He thanks her. He shakes hands with his pal and turns to leave.

(SUGGESTED MUSIC CUE: "MY BUDDY".)

Billy turns back to Ruth and says:

Title Card #12: "I'm sorry. I can't take a job while my pal's starving!"

Billy's Pal looks pathetic. Ruth looks at Billy's Pal and says her father will give them both jobs.

Title Card #13: "Father will give you both jobs!"

Billy and his pal both lift their hats up and down in the air. They jump up and down rejoicing. They kiss Ruth on the cheeks, just as an old janitor enters to dump a pail of dirty water in the street splashing Ruth, Billy and his pal. Billy yells after the old janitor.

Ruth starts to cross the water and Billy stops her. He indicates the ground is all wet. He tells Ruth that he'll take care of it and starts to remove his coat. Ruth turns away, blushing.

Billy looks at the mud, changes his mind, puts his jacket back on and asks his pal for his coat. his pal reluctantly gives him his coat. Billy places it on the ground a la Walter Raleigh.

Ruth steps down on the coat and disappears in the mud. They react.

Fade to black

Title Card #14: "Thickwad screw factory – screwing the American public since 1861."

(SUGGESTED MUSIC CUE: FACTORY WORKER MUSIC. FADE UP: REAR SCREEN PROJECTION: INT. FACTORY OFFICE.)

Billy and his pal ENTER. Standing at a desk in his ornate private office is Brewster Thickwad III, a rich tycoon. Lionel Drippinwithit takes notes. When Brewster sees Billy and his pal, he crosses down. "Yes?"

Title Card #15: "Ruth says you'd give us jobs."

Before Brewster can answer, Lionel takes Billy by the scruff of his collar and kicks him in the seat of his pants.

Brewster calls out, "Wait." Lionel drops Billy, turns back. Billy kicks Lionel in the seats of his pants and steps to his right to adjust his coat, unwittingly changing places with his pal. Lionel reacts to the kick, turns around, sees Billy's Pal and punches him in the face. Lionel turns back to Brewster. Billy kicks Lionel again.

Billy and his pal change places again as Lionel reacts to the kick. He turns back, sees Billy's Pal standing there and socks Billy's Pal a second time. Lionel turns back, Billy kicks him a third time and changes places with his pal a third time.

Lionel reacts to the kick, turns around, and goes to punch Billy's Pal but Brewster grabs his fist. Lionel uses his other hand to bop Billy's Pal in the nose. Brewster says:

Title Card #16: "If my Ruth wants you hired, you're hired! Take them to the assembly line!"

Lionel steps between Billy and Brewster. He hands them overalls, as Billy and his pal lift their hats in the air with glee. They shake hands with each other. Billy reaches across Lionel to shake hands with Brewster. As Lionel turns in Brewster's direction, Billy's Pal kicks Lionel in the backside then poses innocently behind Billy. Lionel turns back and sees Billy. He swings, Billy ducks and Lionel reaches past Billy, socking Billy's Pal anyway.

(REAR SCREEN PROJECTION: WE PAN FROM THE OFFICE IMAGE AS IT MOVES OFF R TO THE FACTORY IMAGE AS IT MOVES ON FROM L AND SETTLES FULL-SCREEN)

Lionel walks Billy and his pal over to a conveyor belt, as the Thickwad office exits S.R. We see two workers robotically twist bolts very slowly on an assembly line. A factory girl walks by with a clip-board. Lionel does lecherous business.

Lionel calls out and Max the Thug ENTERS. He is the foreman. Lionel exits. He explains the job, using a worker: as each bolt rolls out assembly-line style, Billy and his pal will tighten the bolts with their wrenches as they pass by on the conveyor belt. He asks if they under-stand. They say yes. They look at each other as if they'll never be able to do this job right. They get wrenches and just as they get ready to start:

(SUGGESTED MUSIC CUE: LUNCH WHISTLE.)

Billy and his pal wipe their brows and stretch like they're overworked. They see the two workers cross to a bench and sit down for lunch. Billy and his pal rub their stomachs in hunger and watch the Workers eat lunch. They are starving. No one will share. Billy's Pal gets an idea. He sneezes all over the guy's sandwich. The worker disgustedly gives Billy's Pal the sneezed-on sandwich. Billy's Pal devours it.

Billy says "Good idea" and goes up to Worker #2. He sneezes all over the guy's food without even asking for a handout. Worker #2 stares Billy down, then looks out front as he contemplates what to do. He eats the sandwich anyway. Billy tries coughing, spitting and finally hocking up phlegm from his toes. No response. Billy grabs the sandwich, licks both sides of it, then rubs it on his head and rubs it under his armpits. He hands the sandwich back. The worker eats it anyway. Then he reacts.

Title Card #7 "I hate mustard!"

Worker #2 offers Billy the sandwich. Billy takes the disgusting sandwich and shows it to his pal, who grabs it, devours it and reacts. Billy sits, dejected, slapping wrenches together. He looks down and gets an idea. Turning to his pal, He says:

Title Card #18: "If we had two wrenches in each hand, I bet we could do twice as much work."

Billy's Pal asks him to explain. Billy demonstrates, by putting two wrenches in each hand and miming the twisting motion. Billy's Pal still doesn't get it. Billy grabs a napkin and draws his plan out using his pal's back as a drawing table. With each pencil stroke, Billy's Pal gets tickled. When Billy is done, he goes to show his pal the idea and his pal starts tickling him. Billy wards him off and shows him his plan. Billy's Pal says:

Title Card #9: "What a great invention! Show that to the boss! You'll be running this place in no time!"

(SUGGESTED MUSIC CUE: VILLAIN MUSIC.)

Behind their backs, Lionel enters having overheard everything.

Lionel leans over to sneak a peak at the plans. Billy reacts and stuffs them down his pants.

(SUGGESTED MUSIC CUE: LUNCH WHISTLE.)

Lunch is over. Workers go back to the line. Billy and his pal join the others.

Lionel calls Max the Thug over, points to Billy and says:

Title Card #20: "I want what's in his pants."

Max the Thug reacts. Lionel shakes his head and explains. Max gets it, and shakes hands with Lionel sealing the deal, as the factory workers toil behind them.

Fade to black

Title Card #21: "Money would burn holes in their pockets, but they already have holes in their pockets."

(FADE UP: REAR SCREEN PROJECTION: RICH PART OF TOWN.)

Billy and his pal walk down a pleasant street past a freestanding brick wall. They flip coins. Lionel and Max the Thug follow them trying to look inconspicuous. Billy and his pal put the coins in their pockets. Billy's nickel rolls out the bottom of his pants. As it rolls across the ground he bends to retrieve it. Lionel pushes Max towards Billy – now's his chance! As Max reaches for Billy's pocket, Ruth enters. Lionel and Max the Thug quickly hide behind the brick wall. Ruth retrieves the nickel and hands it to Billy.

Title Card #22: "Oh, good. You got the jobs."

Billy and his pal say yes. Billy and Ruth are smitten.

(SUGGESTED MUSIC CUE: LOVE THEME.)

Ruth bites her finger and acts coy. Billy apes her. More shy business. Billy shyly hides his head on his pal's shoulder. Billy sighs, stretches up on his toes and down. Ruth does the same. Billy sighs again and stretches. Ruth and Billy's Pal do the same.

Title Card #23: "I'd ask her out but why would she say yes to a bum like me?"

Ruth waits a beat then says goodbye and turns to walk away. Billy's pal whistles and Ruth turns back, thinking Billy called her. "Yes?" Billy's pal runs behind Ruth to cue Billy in what to say. He mimes "Ask her out." He puts his hand on his stomach and pretends to dance. "Take her dancing." Billy asks Ruth:

Title Card #24: "Do you have a stomach ache?"

Ruth says no as Billy's Pal smacks his own forehead. Billy thinking it's a cue asks Ruth:

Title Card #25: "A cerebral hemorrhage?"

Ruth says no.

Title Card #26: "A fruitcake goes by."

A man with a fruitcake goes by. Billy's Pal runs up behind him and bangs into him. The man reacts. Billy's Pal rips the fruitcake to shreds. The man runs away. Billy's Pal holds up a piece of fruit to Billy. Billy takes it and asks Ruth:

Title Card #27: "Would you like a date?"

She'd be thrilled. Billy's Pal congratulates himself. Ruth and Billy make plans to meet.

Title Card #28: "I'll call for you at eight!"

Ruth shyly waves goodbye and exits. Billy thanks his pal. They shake hands.

Lionel and Max the Thug enter from behind the brick wall and see Billy. Lionel motions to "Get Those Plans!"

Title Card #29: "Get those plans or I'll tell your girlfriend about that night in Toledo!"

Max the Thug looks shocked and guilty.

Title Card #30: "And you thought I was asleep!"

Max the Thug motions he'll get the plans. Lionel EXITS.

Billy and his pal start walking but his pal stops to tie his shoe. As Billy waits, Max the Thug reaches into Billy's left hand pocket and yanks out his boxers. Billy reacts, as Sarge enters and catches them all in the act.

Title Card #31: "You perverts! You'll all rot in jail for this!"

Everyone reacts and attempts to run away, crashing into each other and losing their hats.

Everyone puts hats on their heads. Billy wears Sarge's hat. Max wears Billy's hat. Billy's Pal wears Max's hat. And Sarge wears Billy's Pal's hat. They all react with uproarious laughter.

They hand off their hats clockwise. They now wear the hats handed them. They react to the silliness of it all.

They politely hold the hats they're wearing to their rightful owners then violently drop them to the ground. They bend over to get their hats and bang heads.

Everyone puts on the correct hat. Max takes Sarge's billy club and bops Sarge in the head, handing off the billy club to Billy's Pal. Billy's Pal bops Sarge and EXITS, handing off the club to Lionel. Lionel bops Sarge and exits, handing off the club to Billy. Sarge reacts to Billy, thinking it was him who kept hitting him. He grabs back the club and chases Billy off.

(REAR SCREEN PROJECTION: THE STREET SCENE MOVES.)

As Sarge chases after them off L, the scene behind him and the brick wall move off.

(REAR SCREEN PROJECTION: ALLEY WAY. SUGGESTED MUSIC CUE: CHASE MUSIC.)

From S.R. Billy runs on to C, where he looks both ways to see if the coast is clear. Two cops follow from S.R. and ready their billy clubs to whack him with. Billy backs under their clubs, and they bop each other. Billy sees this and starts to run away S.L. but Sarge and another cop enter from S.L.

Billy is trapped and runs *(In place.)* towards the audience. The cops "follow".

(REAR SCREEN PROJECTION: THE ALLEY SCENE MOVES FARTHER AND FARTHER BACK.)

As Billy runs and the cops follow.

Billy slams into something D.S.C.

Blackout

Title Card #32: "Ouch!"

(LIGHTS UP on: REAR SCREEN PROJECTION: BRICK WALL.)

Billy, his back to the audience, is smashed against the wall. Behind him, we see the cops converge on Billy, clubbing him senseless in a huddle.

Billy crawls out. The cops, meanwhile, continue to club away at nothing.

Title Card #33: "Can't we all just get along?"

Suddenly the cops stop, look at Billy, jump in the air and chase him off R.

(REAR SCREEN PROJECTION: THE ALLEY SCENE MOVES OFF R. REAR SCREEN PROJECTION: STREET SCENE – POOR SIDE OF TOWN MOVES ON FROM R.)

Billy races right back on from S.R., as his wooden fence moves on from the opposite side. They both reach C.S. at the same time.

Billy sees the cops are gaining on him. He ducks behind the fence. Sarge leads the cops in pursuit of Billy. They smash into each other, club each other accidentally, etc.

From behind the fence, Billy pulls down on the top of a plank. The board flies up and catches Sarge between the legs. He motions Billy is behind the fence.

The cops sneak up to the fence, and pull down the top of a plank. When they do, a Billy dummy flies offstage.

The cops follow with their heads and watch horrified as he crashes offstage L. A dowager enters with Billy in her arms, mouthing "Hello, Big Boy." Billy tries to get out of her embrace and sees:

Sarge and the other cops bang their billy clubs into the palms of their hands – in unison. Billy turns back to see the dowager make a kissing face.

Billy looks back and forth between the dowager and the cops. He weighs the pros and cons and then decides to go with the cops. He pries himself loose and from the dowager and dives into the arms of the cops who cart him away, beating him with their clubs.

Title Card #34: "Stood up, Ruth sits."

(REAR SCREEN PROJECTION: Int. Mr. Thickwad's estate.)

Ruth sits. Brewster Thickwad comforts her. The Butler ENTERS and announces:

Title Card #35: "A gentleman caller."

Ruth beams. Brewster tells her she was worried for nothing. The Butler motions in the guest. Lionel Drippinwithit ENTERS, flicking lit ashes into the Butler's outstretched hand. The Butler yelps and exits. We see Ruth's face drop at the sight of Lionel. Lionel says:

Title Card #36: "I took a chance that you'd be free. Dinner?"

He extends his elbow. Ruth and Brewster motion "one moment" to Lionel and turn to each other. Brewster tells her to go ahead. Ruth says "no chance." They turn and smile at Lionel, then go back into their argument. They smile at Lionel again then vehemently fight about this. Finally, Brewster physically makes Ruth takes Lionel's arm. Brewster calls out "Butler!" The Butler ENTERS.

Title Card #37: "Put on her hat and coat!"

The Butler EXITS. Lionel turns to Brewster and says:

Title Card #38: "Don't worry, Mr. Thickwad. You can trust her with me."

Lionel realize he "accidentally" dropped ashes on Ruth's backside. He goes to wipe them off but before he can, the Butler enters wearing a woman's hat & coat. Everyone reacts.

Fade to black

Title Card #39: "Breakin' rocks in the hot sun."

(Fade in: REAR SCREEN PROJECTION: EXT. PRISON YARD.)

Billy's Pal is in prison stripes with three other prisoners. They all break rocks in a jail courtyard, each person hand manacled to a partner.

Sarge shoves in Billy, chained to Max the Thug. Max the Thug paces, dragging Billy back and forth with him. Sarge oversees the prisoners.

Max the Thug gives a nod to the other prisoners. To Billy, Max the Thug whispers:

Title Card #40: "When I give the signal, we're breaking out."

Max the Thug pats his head, rubs his stomach, and moves his legs wildly.

Everyone nods and closes in on Sarge.

(SUGGESTED MUSIC CUE: RIOT SIREN.)

Searchlights circle the yard as Sarge picks up and wields an iron ball on a chain. The Prisoners run in panicked circles around the guard. One by one everyone is smashed in the face or the back of the head with the iron ball. They collapse on top of each other. After a few circles, Billy stops running and motions "after you" to other prisoners, who continue past him to their doom.

(SUGGESTED MUSIC CUE: HARD SMASHES AS THE BALL HITS EACH PRISONER.)

Before he can knock out Billy and Max the Thug, Sarge whips the rope like a lasso and inadvertently knocks himself out with the iron ball. Billy and Max the Thug run in opposite directions, hurting their arms. They run towards each other, smashing into each other. Finally, Billy twirls under Max the Thug's arm like a dance routine and they EXIT together S.L. in a graceful ballet-like exit.

Fade out

(REAR PROJECTION: TENEMENT STREET.)

As Max the Thug walks, Billy is pulled by his hand manacles. He motions they should go back to the jail. Max the Thug says "Shut up." Billy and Max the Thug keep walking. Max the Thug says:

Title Card #41: "Now that I'm free, I'm gonna see my girl."

Billy reacts, as he is pulled across town.

Max the Thug knocks on a tenement door. His girl, a barfly, opens the door and gets knocked in the face. She sees Max and they make eyes. They go to kiss. Attached at the handcuff, Billy spins around and ends up between Max and his girl. Max and his girl kiss Billy instead. Billy reacts.

Max the Thug motions "wait here." He motions "inside." He and his girl ENTER the tenement and slam the door. Billy is jerked against the doorframe by his handcuffed arm. Suddenly his handcuffed arm is pulled up the doorframe. His head is repeatedly slammed against the door. After a beat an exhausted-looking Max and his girl ENTER smoking cigarettes. Billy finds a lit cigarette in his mouth as well. He tosses it away.

Max the Thug says:

Title Card #42: "Get me a saw!"

Max's girl pulls a hacksaw out of her garter. Max saws Billy free and EXITS into the apartment with his girl and the handcuffs as Billy counts his fingers. His pal ENTERS, in his street clothes.

Title Card #43: "Good news. We were pardoned. Here are your pants."

Billy thanks his pal. As he starts to change, he realizes his pal is wearing his pants and Billy has his pal's pants. He motions to his pal, who realizes what he did. They both laugh at their mistake, and pull down their pants - just as a priest walks by. He reacts in horror, and crosses himself. Billy and his pal act embarrassed and pull up their pants. As he EXITS, the priest looks back again for one more peek.

With the coast clear, Billy and his pal attempt to take their pants off a second time, as a fat lady walks by, catching them. She is horrified at seeing men in their underwear and beats them with her purse as Billy and his pal try to pull up their pants. She chases Billy's Pal off.

Billy calls after his pal:

Title Card #44: "Thanks for bringing me my pants!"

Max reacts on the word "Pants." He whispers in his girl's ear. He motions that he wants what's in his pants.

Title Card #45: "I want what's in his pants."

His girl reacts with disgust. Max the Thug reacts to her reaction with even more disgust. He says "No" and whispers in her ear again. She understands and heads for Billy.

The girl looks at Billy seductively and comes at him, swinging her hips and shimmying. When close to Billy, she does one final bump and grind, which makes his hat fly off S.L. Billy turns S.L. to see where his hat went and the girl reaches into his pocket and gets the plans without Billy noticing. Billy turns back to face her.

She shimmies violently, and as he shakes in reaction, his pants fall off.

Max the Thug crosses over and acts outraged. His girl acts innocent, as if Billy is attacking her.

Max the Thug comes at Billy to clobber him. Billy runs with his pants around his ankles, pulling them up as he hides inside the tenement to save Himself. Max holds onto Billy's arm and tries yanking him out of the house.

Title Card #46: "Stand still and fight like an Irishman!"

On the third yank, Billy has been replaced with a Billy dummy. Max slams it to the ground three times. He holds it up and his girl knees it. The dummy flies up in the air, landing with its arms at Max's throat. It chokes him for a beat. Max's girl pulls the dummy off Max and tosses it on the ground. Max and his girl toss it off into the wings S.L.

(REAR SCREEN PROJECTION: THE TENEMENT STREET MOVES OFF R.)

As does Max, his girl, and the doorframe.

(REAR SCREEN PROJECTION: ANOTHER PART OF TOWN MOVES L TO R.)

We see Sarge walking by. He looks up in the air, following a flying body with HIS head from R to L. He EXITS.

(REAR SCREEN PROJECTION: THE OTHER PART OF TOWN MOVES OFF R, AS THE EXT. MR. THICKWAD'S ESTATE MOVES IN FROM L AND SETTLES AT C.)

Billy flies in front of the front door of Brewster Thickwad III's house from off L. He dusts himself off and knocks on the door. The Butler opens the door. Billy says:

Title Card #47: "I'm here for our date."

The Butler, motioning with his finger, asks "You and me?" Billy says no - and motions "with Ruth" - indicated by making the shape of a woman. The Butler says "Oh, of course." He tells him where she is.

Title Card #48: "Ruth is dining with Mr. Drippinwithit."

Billy is horrified. He asks "Where?"

Title Card #49: "Where?"

The Butler answers:

Title Card #50: "Keen's Chophouse."

The title card is upside down. Billy asks him to repeat himself. The Butler looks up, sees the title card and reluctantly stands on HIS head and the card is read right side up.

Title Card #51:"Keen's Chophouse."

Billy thanks him.

Fade to black

Title Card #52: "Keen's Chophouse - The hottest spot in town"

(FADE IN: REAR SCREEN PROJECTION: KEEN'S CHOPHOUSE. SUGGESTED MUSIC: FAST-PACED DANCE MUSIC.)

Patrons in a busy, upscale restaurant, dancing the two-step. Lionel and Ruth are C.S. They drink champagne. Ruth is despondent. Lionel slips a powder from his ring into her drink. Sarge and the dowager are a couple S.L. The lovestruck couple from the opening of the show are S.R. The stuffy French Maitre 'D makes sure everyone is happy.

After a beat of merriment, the stuffy Maitre D' introduces the singing waiter. The waiter removes his apron, drapes it over a chair, and takes over the dance floor to sing.

(A SPOTLIGHT HITS HIM.)

Title Card #53: "A sad song."

(SUGGESTED MUSIC CUE: SAD OPERATIC SONG.)

Everyone listens as the waiter gets up to sing. He sings a very sad song and everyone sobs uncontrollably. Each new verse makes the partons shoulders shake bigger and bigger with uncontrollable sobbing. At the conclusion of the song, water sprays out of a dowager patron's eyes like a faucet.

Everyone applauds the number. Lionel spikes Ruth's drink again, as Billy and his pal sneak in S.R.

Title Card #54: "We've got to find Ruth. I don't trust that Lionel."

They turn to look for Ruth as she collapses facedown. Billy doesn't see her. He goes table to table looking for Ruth. Finally, Billy's Pal see Ruth. As he goes to tell Billy where Ruth is Lionel pours a bottle of champagne into Billy's Pal's pocket. Billy's Pal feels an odd sensation and crosses away thinking he's wet himself.

After his pal EXITS, Billy turns to see Ruth facedown on the table. He is outraged at Lionel and starts to go to him. Lionel sees Billy and has the waiter throw the bum out.

The waiter asks Billy if he has any money. Billy shows the whites of his pockets. The waiter motions "Get out" as he smacks Billy on the chest and points off. Billy rubs his chest and smacks him back. The waiter then shoves Billy, who shoves him back. After several shoves back and forth, The waiter goes to twist Billy's arm behind his back, and spins Billy out of his jacket, which the waiter accidentally puts on inside out. The waiter pushes Billy from the back and accidentally pulls Billy's pants off from the elastic waist and up over his own shoes so that he ends up wearing Billy's pants over his own. Billy is left in his shirt and long johns. He quickly pulls the long apron off the adjoining table and ties it around himself, puts his hat on the waiter and as the "new waiter", Billy has the old waiter *(now dressed in BILLY'S bum clothes.)* thrown out.

Billy's Pal re-enters, stealing food off people's plates.

Billy the waiter goes to Ruth's rescue, but before he gets there, the MAITRE D' calls for him to sing. Billy refuses. The MAITRE D' pushes Billy out to the floor.

(A SPOTLIGHT HITS HIM. SUGGESTED MUSIC CUE: ENGLISH MUSIC HALL QUICK-TEMPO SONG.)

As the music vamps, Billy is forced to sing, which makes everyone laugh so hard they pound the tables and scream. After each verse, Billy motions for his pal to smack Lionel's head with a champagne bottle. Billy's Pal whacks Lionel in the head, but Lionel never notices the pain and keeps laughing up a storm and encouraging Billy to continue with more verses.

At the conclusion of the song, Billy grabs the bottle and swings it over his head, knocking out the Maitre 'D who stands behind him in the process. He clobbers Lionel several times, but Lionel never collapses. Finally, Lionel goes to say something and freezes, his finger extended up as if to make a point. Billy stares at him in his frozen state, waves his hand in front of his face and tries screaming at him to wake him up. Finally, he writes up a check on a dupe pad. He rips off the check, spiking it onto Lionel's finger. Lionel collapses to the floor, knocked out. As Billy and his pal take the unconscious Ruth out, we:

Fade to black

Title Card #55: "In the wee small hours of the morning."

(Fade up: REAR SCREEN PROJECTION: INT. RUTH'S BEDROOM. SUGGESTED MUSIC CUE: LOVE THEME.)

Billy ENTERS with an unconscious Ruth. Billy stands her up in the middle of the floor, and starts to EXIT. Ruth collapses in a heap. Deciding to kiss her goodnight, Billy turns back and trips over Ruth.

Billy tries picking up Ruth's limp body. She is like a jellyfish and she remains unconscious on the floor as her arms slip through his grasp. Billy tries sitting her body up but each time he lets go of her upper torso and runs to reach her feet, she falls back. Finally, he sits her up and then jumps behind her on his knees, clasping her behind the knees. He tries lifting her but cannot budge her. Slowly she tips backwards and they both roll back onto Billy's back, Ruth's legs up in the air.

Billy and Ruth tip over. He finds his foot trapped underneath her. He sits up, and pulls Ruth with his trapped foot back towards the bed.

Billy rolls Ruth off his foot. He lifts Ruth's feet sticking them straight up and kicking himself in the face. His hat falls off. He picks up the hat and hangs it on her foot above his head, thinking it's his head. He stands to remove the hat and her left foot kicks him in the crotch. He reacts.

Billy lifts Ruth up and carries her to the D.S. side of the bed – her head facing the footboard and her feet facing the headboard. He turns around confused as to how to fix the problem. Staying D.S. he spins her the other way, but her feet still face the footboard and her head still faces the footboard.

He realizes his mistake and carries her to the U.S. side of the bed. He lays her on the bed, with her head at the headboard and her feet at the footboard.

He doesn't want her to get cold, so Billy goes to lay the blanket over her. He realizes she is on top of it. He tugs the blanket out from under her, accidentally rolling Ruth off the bed onto the floor D.S. Ruth continues rolling until she is almost off the end of the stage. Billy dives to save her.

Billy sees how far she is from the bed, and gets an idea. He rolls her over once and blows on her. She rolls backwards all the way back to the bed. He picks her up, placing her on the bed.

He places the blanket on her. Content that Ruth's all set, HE blows her a kiss, then tiptoes out. He turns back to tip his hat, then EXITS.

The bed collapses.

Fade to black

(FADE IN: REAR SCREEN PROJECTION: EXT. KEEN'S CHOPHOUSE.)

An old janitor sweeps Lionel Drippinwithit, who rolls over and over himself, into the street. The old janitor never sees him. After the old janitor EXITS, Lionel wakes up, unaware of where he is or how he got there.

Title Card #56: "Where here am I? Where's Ruth? Why are my pants all wet?"

Max the Thug walks by on his way to work. He trips on Lionel and falls. Lionel smacks Max the Thug and pushes him off. Max the Thug realizes it's his boss. He reacts in surprise.

Title Card #57: "You're not gonna believe what I got in my pants!"

He reaches for his pants. Lionel backs away, uninterested in any hanky panky. Max the Thug shakes his head and pulls out Billy's piece of paper. Lionel grabs the paper and reads it with glee.

Title Card #58: "Aha! Billy's sinvention! I'll show him! Nobody treats me like garbage!"

The old janitor re-enters tossing a barrel of fish-heads and bones all over Lionel. As Lionel sputters, the old janitor sweeps Lionel, Max the Thug and all the garbage off S.L.. They barrel roll off.

Fade to black

Title Card #59: "Central Park - where everyone is happy and gay"

(FADE IN: REAR SCREEN PROJECTION: EXT. CENTRAL PARK. SUGGESTED MUSIC CUE: "STROLLING IN THE PARK ONE DAY")

The man with fruitcake rides a bicycle across the stage, stands it up and EXITS. Sarge wakes up a drunk from the park bench and chases him out of the park.

Title Card #60: "Love in bloom"

(SUGGESTED MUSIC CUE: LOVE THEME.)

Billy and Ruth skip into the park from S.R., madly in love. Billy and Ruth stare into each other's eyes and act shy and in love. They skip in opposite circles, waving their hands in the air, winding up in their original positions. Ruth says:

Title Card #61: "Thanks for bringing me home last night. That was so romantic."

Billy reacts.

Title Card #62: "Oh! And I'm sorry I threw up in your hat."

Billy reacts. This is news to him. He drops his hat and slides it away with his foot.

He gets an idea then kneels down before her. He goes to propose and starts to mouth, "will you marry me?" but stops himself when he sadly realizes he has no ring. He runs L and R looking for a ring. He tells her "one moment" looks around and sees a standing bicycle. He unscrews a bolt, and kneels before her. Billy mouths, "Will you marry me?" and grinds the "ring" on her finger.

Ruth accepts. They skip in circles madly in love. Suddenly a newsboy enters.

(SUGGESTED MUSIC CUE: "OVER THERE".)

Title Card #63: "Extra! Extra!"

Billy and Ruth react.

Title Card #64: "America Goes to War!"

A recruiter wheels on an "Uncle Sam Wants You" cart complete sign-up sheets, and tons of patriotic balloons. Max the Thug ENTERS.

Title Card #65: "I'm joining up."

He signs up and gets a uniform, followed by Sarge.

Title Card #6: "So am I."

Others in the park join up as well. Billy realizes he must do his duty. He turns to Ruth and does a dramatic long-winded Patton-like monologue.

Title Card #7: "Me, too."

Billy signs up and gets a uniform. Ruth is impressed.

The man with the fruitcake ENTERS, gets on his bicycle to ride away and his bike collapses underneath him. He looks around for what happened and sees the bicycle bolt on Ruth's finger. He realizes Billy wrecked his bike.

Billy's Pal laughs at his predicament. The man with the fruitcake punches Billy's Pal in the stomach. Billy's Pal reacts and kicks him in the shins.

One by one, Sarge, Max the Thug, the drunk, the Recruiter, join in by tapping someone on the shoulder to see what's wrong, then getting punched in the stomach by the person they tapped and then kicking that person in the shins. A riot takes place with everyone alternately kicking each other in the shins and punching each other in the stomach. A priest ENTERS minding his own business. He too is punched and kicked and joins the fracas.

The riot continues in full speed, segueing to everyone ripping their kicker's pants off, throwing them in the air, kicking everyone else in the shins and punching everyone else in the stomach.

Billy and Ruth hide behind the cart. Finally, the man with the fruit-cake tells everyone to stop. He points to Billy.

Title Card #68: "There's the guy that started it all."

Billy and Ruth find all eyes on them. People rush at Billy to his own shock and surprise, Billy goes straight up in the air attached to the huge bunch of helium balloons. He yells to Ruth:

Title Card #69: "I'll write!"

Ruth waves.

Title Card #70: "I'll wait!"

Everything stops. Everyone hitches in place with jerky repetitive motions. Pops of white light.

(REAR SCREEN PROJECTION: "END OF REEL ONE".)

Curtain

(SUGGESTED MUSIC CUE: "INKY-DINKY PARLEZ VOUS".)

Title Card #71: "France"

Title Card #72: "The Argonne"

Title Card #73: "Called the argonne because most of the men who went there ar gonne now."

(FADE IN: REAR SCREEN PROJECTION: WWI BATTLEFIELD SUGGESTED MUSIC CUE: "OVER THERE".)

In the trenches. Billy's Pal, Sarge, Max the Thug and two other soldiers march on. Billy descends on the same helium balloons, in his uniform, in time to take his place in line.

Sarge calls everyone to attention. "At ease." Everyone lowers his rifle, smashing the foot of the soldier on his right. They drop their guns. Billy picks his up and catches both Max the Thug and Billy's pal in the crotches with his gun. Max gets off, but the nose of the gun is stuck in Billy's pal's butt. Billy tries yanking it free then falls as his pal walks in a circle, gun attached to his butt. Finally, Billy puts his foot on his pal's back and yanks the rifle. It comes free. Billy looks at the gun for moment then switches guns with his pal.

The Sarge calls the men to attention. He calls them to "About face." All the soldiers turn correctly, except for Billy. He steps in front of his left foot with his right, and then twists backwards with an upraised arm.

Sarge not quite sure he saw what he thought he saw, makes them all "About face" again. Again, everyone but Billy does it correctly. Sarge shakes his head and orders them to "Halt." And "At ease."The soldier delicately rest their guns on the ground, careful not to get their feet smashed by the others' rifles.

Sarge calls Billy over. Sarge yells "About face!" Billy does his version. Sarge orders it again. Billy turns again.

Sarge, clearly frustrated, tries to teach Billy "about face" by demonstrating the first part of the move - you put your right foot behind your left. Billy shows how he does it - with HIS right foot over his left. Sarge says no and demonstrates again. Billy demonstrates his way. Sarge says no, and keeps doing the same step over and over, unconsciously segueing into a Charleston.

(SUGGESTED MUSIC CUE: "CHARLESTON".)

Sarge recovers and drops to his knees, grabbing Billy's right leg and pumping it, while explaining verbally what he wants. Billy thinks he's flirting with him. He explains he doesn't go for that sort of thing and motions for him to move away. He suggests Sarge might find what he's looking for with one of the other soldiers.

Sarge, getting more and more frustrated, kicks Billy's leg. Billy kicks him back. Sarge kicks him again. Billy kicks him back. Sarge tries a really big kick and Billy lifts his leg. Sarge swings, misses and falls on the ground. Billy offers his hand to help him up and as Sarge reaches for it, Billy is distracted by one of the soldiers. He turns, pulling his hand away. Sarge falls again. Everyone laughs at him. From the ground in front of Billy he motions "Shoulder arms!"

Billy jerks his rifle up and over his shoulder, knocking Sarge in the face with his gun as he does. Sarge crawls S.L. and orders "About face!" This time, everyone does Billy's version of an about face - slapping their left thigh, stepping over their left leg with their right leg and then twisting backwards with an upraised arm. As Sarge reacts, the men daisychain off R. Sarge dances off.

Fade out

Title Card #74: "Ruth pines for her doughboy"

(FADE IN: REAR SCREEN PROJECTION: INT. MR. THICKWAD'S ESTATE.)

A picture of Billy in uniform sits on the table, as Ruth cries into a handkerchief, then wrings it out on the floor. Water pours from the handkerchief.

Lionel ENTERS with his cigar in his mouth. He slips on the water and falls on his face, smashing the cigar. He throws the cigar violently off L. The Butler ENTERS behind him with a silver tray filled with mail. He has Lionel's smashed cigar in his mouth. He acts surprised, then takes the cigar out of his mouth and tosses it off L.

Before Ruth sees him, Lionel thanks the Butler, tips him to go away, and takes the mail. The Butler EXITS. Lionel steals his cash back, with a dollar-on-a-wire gag.

Behind Ruth's back Lionel rummages through the mail.

Title Card #75: "Curses! A letter from Billy!"

Lionel stuffs the letter from Billy into his jacket. He hands the rest of the mail to Ruth. She sees no letter from Billy and cries.

Title Card #76: "Six months and still no word from Billy!"

Lionel acts outraged.

Title Card #77: "That cad! And after all those letters I mailed for you!"

Lionel gleefully opens his jacket so only the audience can see. It is lined with all her letters to Billy. He laughs maniacally.

Fade to black

Title Card #78: "HOMESICK BLUES"

(FADE IN: REAR SCREEN PROJECTION: WWI BATTLEFIELD.)

Billy looks at a framed photo, sighs and turns the photo around. It's Ruth. A soldier looks at a framed photo, sighs and turns the photo around. It's his girl from home. Another soldier looks at a framed photo, sighs and turns the photo around. It's a picture of a horse. His pal looks at a framed photo and sighs. Billy looks over at the picture, takes it, and turns it right-side up. He hands it back to his pal, who wasn't aware her photo was upside down. He reacts in horror. He shows the photo to the soldiers, who react in horror.

Sarge ENTERS. The mail's in. The Soldier and Billy's Pal get letters and packages from home. Not Billy. He gets nothing. Sarge starts to EXIT. Billy calls for Sarge. Didn't he get any mail? Sarge says no.

Title Card #79: "Maybe next month, son."

Sarge EXITS. Billy tries to reads over the other's shoulders. They push him away. Billy stands alone, as all the others read and laugh and eat. Billy sobs silently.

Sarge enters with the mailbag. He motions one more letter. Billy dries his eyes and starts for Sarge. Sarge motions it's for one of the others. The Soldier who loves horses steps forward and gets a horseshoe. The soldier whinnies and counts with his foot and he stares at the horse's photo and the horseshoe. Billy reacts.

Title Card #80: "As our boys fight over there, old men and flat-footed Lionel run the country over here."

(FADE IN: REAR SCREEN PROJECTION: INT. THICKWAD SCREW FACTORY.)

The factory is empty except for Brewster, Lionel and two old bearded men workers. Brewster is noticeably upset. He rips out some of his own hair in frustration.

Title Card #81: "The war has left us short-handed."

We see one of the old bearded workers only has one hand. Lionel tells Brewster not to worry. He pulls out two "double wrenches." Everyone is impressed. The old bearded men workers use their new double-wrenches to great success. Lionel beams. Brewster shakes his hand. Brewster to Lionel:

Title Card #82: "Your new invention will save the company, Lionel! How can I ever repay you?"

Ruth ENTERS. Lionel smiles his lecherous smile.

Title Card #83: "Give me your company and let me marry Ruth so I can use her as a vessel for my evil spawn!"

Ruth and Brewster react in shock. Lionel sees them looking at him.

Title Card #84: "Oh. Did I say that out loud?"

Ruth announces:

Title Card #85: "I'll never marry you. I'm waiting for Billy."

Lionel gets an idea and says:

Title Card #86: "I didn't want to tell you this... but... Billy is dead! Shot in the back as he ran from a fight."

Ruth collapses in tears in her father's arms. Lionel laughs maniacally.

Fade to back

Title Card #87: "Gambling for their lives"

The soldiers play rock-paper-scissor as Sarge ENTERS carrying two rifles.

Title Card #88: "One of our guys has been captured!"

Everyone reacts with horror.

Title Card #89: "I need two voluntees to save Private Ryan!"

Sarge motions take two steps forward. Everyone takes two steps backwards. Sarge motions two steps forward. They take another step backward. The two soldiers trick Billy and his pal by running forward and then stepping back just as Billy and his pal get to the front of the line. Sarge congratulates them, and hands them rifles. One soldier asks Billy's pal if he can have his shoes after he's killed. Everyone waves goodbye and walk backwards off R. Billy and his pal take their rifles and set out.

Billy and his pal walk in place, as the backdrop behind them moves from the bunker into a forest scene.

(REAR SCREEN PROJECTION: WE PAN FROM THE AMERICAN BUNKER AS IT MOVES OFF R TO A FOREST AS IT MOVES ON FROM L. LIGHTING CHANGES TO BATTLE/EXPLOSION EFFECTS.)

As they walk *(In place.)* through the forest, Billy and his pal are caught in crossfire. They fire and keep walking.

(REAR SCREEN PROJECTION: PAN FROM THE FOREST AS IT MOVES OFF R TO THE ENEMY BUNKER AS IT MOVES ON FROM L.)

A bearded German paces around a captured Max.

Title Card #90: "How do you vant to die?"

Max the Thug answers:

Title Card #91: "After you!"

They laugh at the joke. Behind them, Billy tries shooting the enemy soldier in the back but his gun is jammed. He stamps his foot as he pulls the trigger a second time. Still jammed. Billy's Pal tries shooting the enemy soldier, too, but his rifle is backwards.

The enemy soldier begins to raise his gun to kill Max. Billy bangs the butt of the gun on the ground in frustration to un-jam the gun. The rifle goes off. A goose falls from the sky clocking the enemy soldier in the head and knocking him unconscious.

They react. Max is freed. Pal grabs the enemy soldier by the foot and Billy, Max, Pal and the unconscious enemy soldier "run" back from the enemy bunker through the woods to the American bunker.

(REAR SCREEN PROJECTION: FAST-SPEED PAN FROM THE ENEMY BUNKER THROUGH THE FOREST SETTLING ON THE AMERICAN BUNKER AS IT MOVES ON FROM R.)

In time with the projection, Sarge and the two soldiers run on from off R and meet Billy, Pal, Max and the unconscious enemy at C. Everyone congratulates Billy. Max says:

Title Card #92: "Billy is the bravest man of all!"

Sarge goes to pin a medal on Billy. Billy faints at the sight of the stickpin.

Fade to black

(FADE IN: REAR SCREEN PROJECTION: INT. MR. THICKWAD'S ESTATE.)

Ruth wears widow's weeds, holding Billy's photo. Lionel is on his knees proposing. He whips out a huge diamond ring. Ruth takes one last look at Billy's photo, kisses it, and then turns it face down on the table. She rises to say:

Title Card #93: "Okay. I'll marry you. But not because I love you. But because you're the only man I know who's still alive."

Lionel says:

Title Card #94: "Good enough for me."

He dips her back for a congratulatory kiss and sticks his tongue out, as we:

Fade to black

Title Card #5: "A hero's welcome."

(FADE IN: SUGGESTED MUSIC CUE: "WHEN JOHNNY COMES MARCHING HOME" REAR SCREEN PROJECTION: POOR SIDE OF TOWN.)

Billy as he walks back to his "home."

Title Card #96: "Home sweet home"

(SUGGESTED MUSIC CUE: "BE IT EVER SO HUMBLE THERE'S NO PLACE LIKE HOME".)

Billy heads for his spot behind the fence. A bum steps out and yells at Billy to get lost. Billy apologizes, and sadly pulls out a "VET" sign and starts begging.

A dowager with a black and white dog enters. She sees the sign and asks, "Are you a Vet?" Billy says yes. She asks him to look at her dog's paw. Billy explains he's not that kind of "Vet." He extends the rest of the sign that reads: "VET-ERAN." The dowager walks away.

Sarge appears. He and Billy are happy to see each other. They salute each other and then hug. Sarge asks what he's up to now. Billy says, "Nothing." Sadly he shows his empty pockets, saying he has nowhere to live. No food. He asks if Sarge can spare a crumb.

Sarge feels bad then reacts.

Title Card #97: "So, you're still a bum!"

The cop in Sarge takes over and he clubs Billy.

The other bum rolls out from under the fence. Sarge drops Billy and chases the bum away, clubbing him. Billy calls after them.

Title Card #98: "And stay out!"

(SUGGESTED MUSIC CUE: "MY BUDDY".)

Billy starts to crawl back under his fence as his pal ENTERS and whistles. Billy reacts as if deafened by the sound. His pal says:

Title Card #99: "Come with me! You're not going to believe this!"

Billy reacts and they run off.

Fade out

Title Card #100: "Will everyone please rise?"

(FADE IN: REAR SCREEN PROJECTION: INT. CHURCH. SUGGESTED MUSIC CUE: "HERE COMES THE BRIDE".)

Brewster walks Ruth down the aisle. Ruth is in a wedding dress, Lionel in tails. A priest is at the altar. Sarge, a Bridesmaid, the fruitcake man and a fat lady are the guests. A "JUST MARRIED" suitcase sits U.S.L. The fat lady holds a Terrier. Everyone faces the Priest U.S. Billy runs in from S.R. with his pal, thinking he's too late. Billy sees Ruth and clearly mouths "Holy Shit!" A beat after he mouths it:

Title Card #101: "OH NO!"

Billy's Pal tells Billy to stop the wedding but Billy shakes his head and sadly says:

Title Card #102: "No wonder she never wrote. What would she want with a bum like me?"

Billy turns away and cries. Everyone turns to shush him. Ruth sees him, cries out.

Title Card #103: "Billy!"

All are deafened.

Title Card #104: "Lionel told me you were dead!"

Billy reacts.

Title Card #105: "Well, nobody told me!"

Lionel grabs Ruth. Billy grabs her back.

A tug of war starts, as one by one the wedding guests grab opposing sides. A mini-conga starts.

(SUGGESTED MUSIC CUE: "BRAZIL".)

Finally, Lionel and Billy pull at the same time, stretching Ruth's arms ten feet wide. Everyone lets go. The rubber hands shoot back and hit Ruth in the head as everyone else topples to the ground in various positions.

Billy grabs Ruth. They jump in the air and run out of the church S.R. Brewster screams:

Title Card #106: "After that bum! He's got my daughter!"

(SUGGESTED MUSIC CUE: CHASE MUSIC.)

Everyone jumps in the air and runs after them off R. The fat lady carries the "JUST MARRIED" suitcase.

(REAR SCREEN PROJECTION: STREET SCENE – OUTSIDE CHURCH. SUGGESTED MUSIC CUE: CHASE MUSIC.)

Billy and Ruth run from S.L. to S.R. – chased by everyone else. Billy's Pal is the last in line. He stops at C, looks off R, reacts then runs off R. Everyone follows R to L in a panic. Billy and Ruth are last.

(REAR SCREEN PROJECTION: STREET SCENE – A TRAIN MOVES ACROSS THE SCREEN FROM R TO L. REAR SCREEN PROJECTION: DIFFERENT STREET SCENE.)

Billy runs on L to R holding Ruth's hand. He lets go in time to motion "this way" just as Lionel ENTERS from S.R. throws Ruth over his shoulder and EXITS S.L. Billy's Pal rides a bike S.R. to S.L in hot pursuit.

The Priest chases the Bridesmaid from S.L. to S.R.

(REAR SCREEN PROJECTION: MOVING SLIDE OF POOR SIDE OF TOWN.)

The slide moves on with Billy's fence, as the fat lady enters S.L. carrying her dog and the suitcase.

As the fat lady and the wall reach C.S. the slide settles and freezes in place.

Lionel ENTERS from S.R. dragging a resistant Ruth. He turns, accidentally knocking into the fat lady. They fall with the dog between them. Ruth flees behind the fence.

Lionel rises. He picks up the dog, pets it, and then dropkicks it off S.L. Lionel EXITS off S.R. looking for Ruth. The fat lady EXITS S.L. looking for her dog.

Billy's Pal skates on from S.L. Sarge follows with the fat lady's dog attached to his shin. He clubs it as he runs, missing the dog and hitting his leg. They EXIT S.R.

Billy ENTERS from S.R. calling for Ruth. Ruth ENTERS from behind the fence.

Title Card #107: "Billy! Save me! Hide Me!"

Billy gets an idea. He leans the fat lady's suitcase against the wall and opens it. Ruth dives into the fat lady's suitcase. Billy closes it up and starts to carry it away, when Lionel ENTERS. They struggle for possession of the suitcase as SARGE enters.

He clubs Billy.

Billy's Pal breaks it up:

Title Card #108: "Stop! You're beating the wrong man!"

Sarge and Lionel start beating Billy's Pal. Billy's Pal stops them.

Title Card #109: "Let me tell you the whole story!"

Everyone ENTERS and listens. Billy's Pal acts out the entire play in thirty seconds. When done, a confused Brewster deadpans, "What?"

Billy's Pal points up to the title card. Brewster looks up, then crosses D.S. looks back up at the title cards and reads with his back to the audience. Everyone's heads bob in unison following Brewster as he reads the cards.

Title Card #110: "Billy invented the double-wrench! Lionel stole the plans and took all the credit! And then he told Ruth Billy was dead just so he could marry her!"

Brewster gets it now. Brewster crosses back to Billy's Pal.

Title Card #111: "Well, why didn't you just say so?"

Billy's Pal reacts. Brewster says to Billy:

Title Card #112: "Your wrench saved my factory! And your bravery saved our country! Welcome aboard...partner, or should I say... 'son'!"

Brewster shakes Billy's hand. As people cheer, Lionel slinks off R, using the suitcase as a shield. Billy is made a hero. People toss him up in the air and cheer.

Title Card #113: "Hooray!

More cheering and tossing Billy in the air.

Title Card #114: "Yippee!"

More cheering and tossing Billy in the air. The fruitcake man steps forward, as Billy's "real" body is switched for a "Billy Dummy." The fruitcake man says:

Title Card #115: "That is one firm bum!"

People cheer and toss "Billy" straight up. He never comes down. Everyone stands with their arms straight up in the air. After a beat, they lower their arms and raise them up again, as if that will make the body come back down. Then keeping their arms extended, they lower their hands and raise them again. One by one, they look guilty and scatter.

After everyone EXITS, "Billy" falls to earth, behind the wall.

Billy's Pal ENTERS as Billy comes around the wall.

Title Card #116: "Where's Ruth?"

Billy indicates the suitcase. It is gone! Billy asks: "Where did she go?" His Pal doesn't know. Billy motions "You look that way" *(S.R.)* and "I'll look that way" *(S.L.)*.

They look off for Ruth, can't find her, and meet at C switching positions. Billy motions "Okay, this time, you look over there." He motions S.L.

A BAKER carrying two pies enters from S.R.

Billy continues, "And I'll look that way." Billy motions to the R on "that" and accidentally shoves the baker's pie into the baker's face. Billy never sees him and continues looking off R for Ruth. The baker reacts. Billy's Pal laughs at The baker's misfortune. The baker slams the other pie into Billy's Pal's face, and EXITS off R.

Billy returns to C and sees his pal covered in white goo. He looks up in the sky to see what kind of bird did the damage.

Billy moves L to look for Ruth as The baker returns from S.R. with a large cart of pies. He sets it at C.S. and gets two more pies as Billy crosses S.R. looking for Ruth. The baker follows behind with two pies.

Sarge enters from S.R. as The baker throws the first pie and Billy leans out of the way. Sarge gets it in the face. The baker runs back to the cart, shoving a pie in Billy's Pal face as he goes.

Across the stage, the man with the fruitcake ENTERS, asks Billy's Pal what happened. Billy's Pal slams him in the face with a pie.

As Sarge reacts to his face full of pie, Billy rises to see him covered in goo. He looks up to see the bird that did this. Sarge returns with two pies, as The baker sneaks up on Billy.

Billy sees the pies coming from both sides and ducks. The baker and Sarge duck with him. Billy rises. They rise as well. Billy ducks. They stay up. He rises. As they go to hit him with the pies, Billy gestures "I give up" knocking into the pies with his hands which in turn hit the baker and Sarge in the face with their own pies.

Meanwhile, the bridesmaid ENTERS from S.L. sees what's happening and tries to EXIT the way she came in. As she turns to go, she is hit in the backside with a pie. She turns back to see who hit her and gets another in the face.

The fruitcake tries crawling away to S.R. Sarge hits him in the face and the baker gets him in the backside.

As the chaos grows, the priest ENTERS, piously telling everyone to stop immediately. There is a beat then he is slammed in the head with two pies like they are cymbals. A barrage of pies hit him and he goes down like Sonny Corleone in the "Godfather" tollbooth scene. A beat after he lies motionless, Billy's Pal picks up the Priest's head and drops it in a pie he sets on the floor below his face.

A free-for-all breaks out. In the midst of the chaos, Lionel enters from S.R. trying to cross the stage hidden by the suitcase. Everything stops. En masse, the Angry Mob changes directions, turns and goes to pummel Lionel to death, carrying him off R.

Billy is left alone. He looks off R and off L, and feels lost.

Title Card #117: "A job and a future and it all means nothing without Ruth."

He sits on the suitcase D.S.C.

Title Card #118: "Ouch, you're sitting on my head!"

Billy realizes where the voice is coming from. He opens the suitcase and Ruth pops out. They go to kiss.

(SUGGESTED MUSIC CUE: LOVE THEME.)

Ruth says:

Title Card #119: "There's so much I want to say..."

Billy answers:

Title Card #120: "Sometimes you don't need words."

They go to kiss and see the audience. They hide themselves behind Billy's hat, as we iris down and:

Fade to black

Title Card #121: "THE END"

(SUGGESTED MUSIC CUE: CRESCENDO ENDING.)

SILENT LAUGHTER

CURTAIN FALLS

End of play

CURTAIN CALL

Consists of a speeded up chase with everyone chasing after Lionel. Actors stop to bow along the way and then continue the chase. Additional actors are added as the chase goes on, each stopping to take their bows at the appropriate times.

After the company bow, everyone acknowledges the organist.

Billy steps forward and raises his hands asking everyone for silence. He steps forward to make a curtain speech and mouths:

Title Card #122: "Thank you."

Billy steps back, joins the Company for another bow and...

CURTAIN FALLS

SILENT LAUGHTER

PRODUCTION NOTES

Obviously "Silent Laughter" can be done as simply or as complicated as your budget allows. Listed below are a few "tricks" to make the show as easy as possible to produce.

* The organ accompanies the action, not the other way around. This is not a ballet. Use original music or public domain period music from 1917.

* The roles can be broken up in any way that befits your production. You can do this show with ten people or ten thousand. A cast of nine is possible, but will kill your actors and your dressers.

* All action on stage should freeze when dialogue title cards are projected over the actors' heads, except for the person speaking. The person speaking should mouth the lines directly out front for as long as it takes someone to read the card from the audience.

* Don't over complicate the gags. Some of the best silent movie gags were done with cheap-looking dummies and string.

* Breathe. Actors have a tendency to hold their breath when trying to be "silent."

* There is plenty of dialogue in each scene – we just can't hear it. Feel free to "speak" *(mouth the lines.)* in character during your scenes.

* Close your mouth during the pie fight.

* If there are no escapes behind the fences: Billy can escape from behind the free-standing stockade fence in the "cop chase scene" by having two cops exit behind the fence at S.R. and re-enter from behind the fence S.L. to see where the flying dummy flew to, when it flew OFF L. One of the cops stays behind the fence and is replaced by Billy wearing a cop hat over his own costume and his back to the audience. Likewise, after the "suitcase gag," Ruth can escape from behind the fence under the fat lady's dress when everyone looks up to see where the dummy went. Just position the fat lady to stand next to the fence as she looks up, have Ruth duck underneath and walk off with her.

* The crying gag is done with a hot water bottle filled with water, attached to the wig with tubing. The actor squeezes the hot water bottle to make the "crying effect."

* The suitcase bit is a vaudeville gag from Buster Keaton's "Sherlock Junior." The suitcase is rigged with two hinged doors at the back. The inside of the suitcase is covered in black with extra clothes hanging inside to mask the exit. For the gag, the suitcase is placed against the stockade fence. Once the suitcase is in place, the stockade fence's hidden trap door is opened behind the fence by a crew member. Ruth dives through the suitcase and out the back of the fence – unseen by the audience. The trap is instantly closed and the suitcase is lifted away from the wall creating a split second disappearance effect.

* The bicycle is a regular bike with removable handlebars that are detached by a pin. The actor controls his own fall.

* Use shaving cream for the pies to save your costumes. We used Gillette Foamy which withstood the stage lights and sitting around for long periods of time.

SET PIECES/RIGGED GAGS

Street:
Free-standing Stockade Fence – with a hidden panel for the suitcase gag and a pivoted plank for Billy's entrance and the Dummy Gag
Pram Rigged with Squirt Bottle
Trap Door with Elevator Drop

Factory:
Table
Bench
Freestanding Conveyor Belt
(Operated Manually with Crank Handle, Internally, Two Speeds)

Street:
Dummy Rig, Flown USC Behind Fence (Up and Down)
Freestanding Brick Wall

Thickwad Estate:
Chair
Pedestal Table

Tenement Street:
Freestanding Door Frame - Low Income

Ext. Thickwad Estate:
Freestanding Door Frame - Elaborate

Keen's Chophouse:
3 Cafe Tables
6 Cafe Chairs
Dowager Wig Rigged with Hoses

Ruth's Bedroom:
Freestanding Collapsible Bed
Chair

Central Park:
Collapsible Bicycle w/Pin
"Uncle Sam Wants You" Recruiter Cart
Small Park Bench
Flying Balloon Rig U.S.L. (Flown Straight Up and Down)

Street:
Rigged Suitcase (Hinged Door Back)
Pie Cart with 100 pies

SILENT LAUGHTER

COSTUME PLOT

(Entirely in Shades of Black, Grey and White)

NOTE: All clothing pieces should be derived from styling from the years of 1910-1917

BILLY
Weathered tailcoat
Oversized duplicate trick tailcoat
Round-tip collared shirt, tie and vest
Period trousers with trick pockets
Oversized duplicate trick trousers
Long johns
Black beat-up derby

RUTH
1917 White Lace tea dress with pantaloons, stockings, white gloves
1917 Satin wrap dress for Keen's Chophouse, with hair ornament
1917 Wrap front lightweight walking coat, matching gloves, small straw hat
Black silk mourning dress
1917 Wedding dress with trick arms, and veil

BILLY'S PAL
Weathered suit coat with velvet collar
Charcoal long-John Henley
Plaid trousers with suspenders
Duplicate break-away trousers
Long johns
Beat up hat
Convict uniform and hat
World War I Coat

LIONEL
Black slick Double breasted suit with velvet trim
White pique front shirt
Satin vest and Ascot
Spats
Wedding vest and Ascot for Second Act

BREWSTER THICKWAD III
Morning coat with braided rim
White Satin vest and bow tie
Ribbed front shirt
Silver pocket watch on chain
Grey pinstripe plain front trousers
Wool top hat

SARGE
Black tunic coat uniform with banded collar
White tab shirt
Patrolman's belt
Keystone Helmet
Black pants
Duplicate black rip-away pants
Long Johns

MAX THE THUG
A-line t-shirt with false chest hair
Baggy tweed trousers with suspenders
Leather cap

MAX'S DAME
Black lace camisole
Grey silk wrap tunic trimmed with fur

Black walking skirt
Lace garter

BUTLER
Cutaway tuxedo
Vest
Ribbed front shirt with bow tie

FAT LADY//MOTHER
Grey print day dress with gathered waistline, and ruffled bosom
Pantaloons
Purse
White wool hat with doves

SINGING WAITER
Ribbed front shirt with plain collar
Black satin bowtie
Black Tuxedo pants
Leather braces and suspenders
Oversized Bistro Apron

FRUITCAKE MAN/MAN ON BIKE
Holloway jacket
Wing tip shirt
Polka dot Bow tie
Bold plaid vest
Houndstooth trousers, and Break-away trousers
Long johns
Straw boater

PRIEST
Waist seamed coat with clerical collar
Trousers

Plain long johns
Brimmed parson's hat

DRUNK
Ill-fitted trench coat
Wingtip collared shirt
Bow tie
Wool vest with pockets
Trousers
Duplicate Breakaway trousers
Long johns
Dented grey derby

VENDOR
Striped button collar shirt
Linen overalls
Three button hopsack jacket
Derby

MAITRE'D
Single button wool suit
Black satin vest
Ribbed front shirt with bow tie

NEWSBOY
Argyle sweater
Round collared shirt
Tweed Knickers
Tweed newsboy cap

JANITOR
Linen overalls
Striped button collar shirt

SILENT LAUGHTER

Beat up brimmed hat

DOWAGER
Long Black lace dress with skirted peplum
Shawl
Two toned brimmed straw hat

LOVESTRUCK GIRL
White peaked collar blouse
Satin waist sash
Diagonal striped shirt
Grey straw skimmer hat with flowers

LOVESTRUCK BOY
Three buttoned plaid jacket
High Round-tip collared shirt
Striped long tie
White plain front trousers
High Derby

FACTORY GIRL
Two toned grey dress with peplum with appliqu? and buttons

RECRUITER
WWI Uniform with break-away slacks
Military hat
Long johns

KEYSTONE COPS
Black tunic coat with mandarin collar, and trousers
White tab shirt
Keystone helmet with badge

CONVICTS
Black and white wide striped buttoned front shirt and matching baggy pants
cap

WWI SOLDIERS
WWI American tunic coat and field pants, with leg wrappings
Field Helmet

ENEMY SOLDIER
Grey wool WWI German jacket and pants
Utility belt
Spiked top German field hat
Over the calf boots

WORKERS
Plaid collared shirt
Grey linen flannel overalls with patch
Distressed apron
Wool cap

OLD WORKERS
Print long sleeved shirt
Trousers
Distressed Apron
Cap

SILENT LAUGHTER

PROPERTY LIST

(Entirely in Shades of Black, Grey and White)

Vendor's Push Cart
Frying Pan
Tongs
Towel
Plate
Pastries (5)
String of Sausage (Cloth)
Baby Stroller
Cigar
Umbrella
Bucket
Factory Worker Aprons (4)
Large Wrenches (4)
Lunch Pails (2)
Sandwiches (2)
Cloth Napkins (2)
Pencil
Fruitcake
Date
Plate
Men's Underwear
4 Billy Clubs
4 Mustaches
2 Cloth "Billy" Look-alike Dummies (One for Rig, One Free-Standing)
Tetherball and Chain
Rubber (Reinforced) Hand Manacles (3 Sets)
2 Sledgehammers
Hacksaw

Door Mat
Tic Tacs (white)
Cigar
2 Exploded Cigars
Pocket Watch and Chain
6 Wine Glasses
2 Wine Bottles
1 Rubber Wine Bottle
6 Place Settings
Dupe Pad
Pencil
Champagne Bucket with Stand
Broom
Barrel of Garbage, i.e. Fish-heads, Bones and Shoes
Collapsible Bicycle w/Pin
Clip-Board
Pencil
30 Helium Balloons
Cart
6 Doughboy Helmets
5 Rifles
2 German Helmets
Photo of Ruth
Photo of Fat Woman
Photo of Horse
3 Bundles of Mail
Mail Bag
2 "Double Wrenches"
Crepe Hair (to Match Brewster Thickwad)
Silver Tray
Mail
Photo of Billy
Handkerchief

SILENT LAUGHTER

Goose
Medal
Stickpin
"Veteran" Sign
Bride's Bouquet
Bridesmaid Bouquet
Terrier Dog (2)
Trick Suitcase
Rollerskates
Pie Cart
Shaving Cream, 4 pies per can (Gillette Foamy worked best for us)
Cardboard Pie Pans

SILENT LAUGHTER

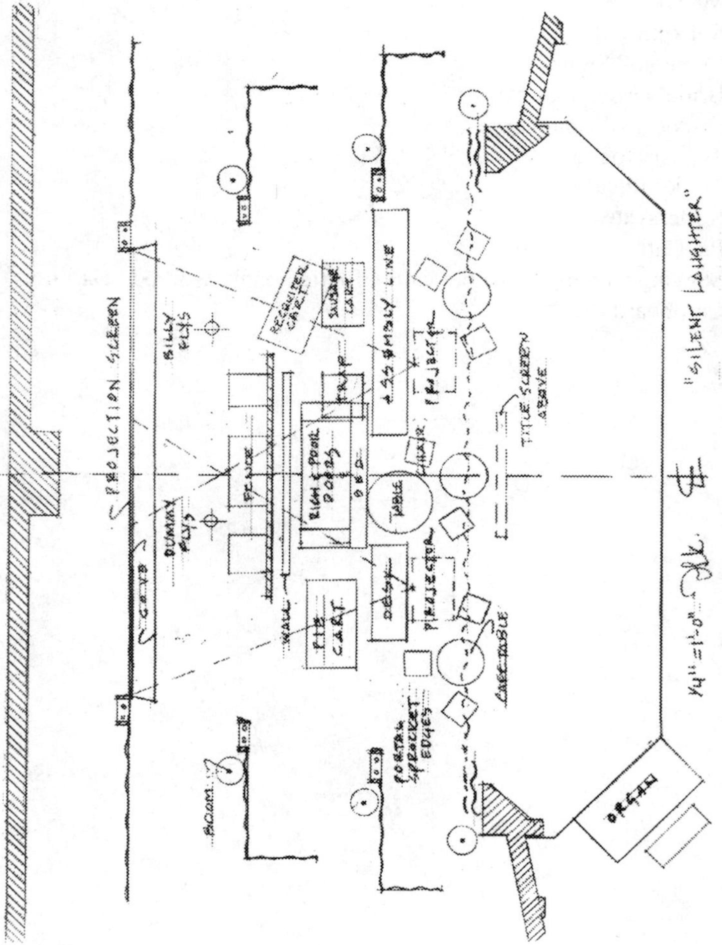

SILENT LAUGHTER -- Composite Ground Plan
Set Design by Dana Kenn

Flight
ARTHUR GIRON

"A witty, touching flashback…There is poignancy between the laughs." —*The New York Times*

The author doesn't claim it happened exactly this way. He has taken real-life characters and biographical information and supposed what it was like for Orville and Wilbur growing up in the dysfunctional Wright family. They are portrayed as boys whose mischief is just a sign of frustrated brilliance. Not a documentary, the play explores the dynamics of the Wright family in theatrical terms. 4 m., 1 f. (#8179)

Pride's Crossing
TINA HOWE

Best American Play of 1998
New York Drama Critics Circle

"A play you will remember and forever cherish.…It is rich in both texture and imagination."— *New York Post*

"A lovely achievement…Mabel becomes a woman who ... both typified her time and her class and transcended it."—*Variety*

At ninety, Mabel Tidings Bigelow insists on celebrating her daughter and granddaughter's annual visit with a croquet party. As the party unfolds, she relives vignettes from the past that reveal the precise moment of opportunity lost and love rejected that define her life. The vibrant portrait of Mabel that takes shape culminates in her one shining achievement when she became the first woman to swim the English Channel. 4 m., 3 f. (#18230)

Send for your copy of the Samuel French
BASIC CATALOGUE OF PLAYS AND MUSICALS